Contents

PART 1 GENERAL

PART 2 PRACTICE
Planning & Review Forms

The Records

PART 3 – MANAGEMENT

NB. *Material in this guide is based, primarily on the DH*
"Training Resources Pack". It takes account of the latest
revised Consultation Papers and Planning and Review
forms, of feedback from local authorities and of
monitoring undertaken by the DH. Sincere thanks are
due to the DH Social Services Inspectors and members
of the LAC Implementation Team for their support.
Any errors or omissions are the sole responsibility of
the author.

Re-printed 2004

PART 1 GENERAL

Introduction

This guide is designed for use by all those in England and Wales, who plan, manage and/or deliver services to individual children and young people looked after away from home. This includes councillors, managers, social workers, residential social workers and foster carers.

It is presented in a style which will support an understanding and use of the *Looking After Children: Good Parenting, Good Outcomes* (LAC) material which is now in use in over 90% of local authorities.

The guide should be used to build on and reinforce Department of Health (DH) guidance, eg. its 1995 Training and Resource Pack, the Performance Assessment Framework and Quality Protects.

In using the LAC system, readers need also to take into account local authority policy and practice expectations which should be found in Children's Services Plans, child care policy statements and in agency procedures.

Principles & Values of LAC

The *Looking After Children: Good Parenting, Good Outcomes*
(LAC) system was developed in parallel with the
implementation of the Children Act 1989 and has incorporated
the philosophy, principles and values of the Act in the
following way:

- Welfare of the child/young person is paramount
- Need for corporate parents to aim for standards
  equivalent to those of a well-informed parent with
  adequate resources
- Corporate parents need formal systems to plan and
  record what good parents keep in mind
- Those with case responsibility must work in partnership
  with birth parents, current carers and relevant other
  professionals
- A child/young person must be consulted and listened to
  as soon as they are old enough
- Each child/young person is an individual with unique
  needs
- A child/young person with a disability is first and
  foremost a child/young person who has additional needs
- Contact with parents and extended family is to be
  encouraged and supported unless specific reasons/court
  orders justify not so doing
- A child/young person has a right to be kept in touch with
  their birth family's religious and cultural traditions
  directly or indirectly

- The overall aim of looking after children/young people away from home is to promote well-being and success, not just to prevent harm

- Whilst looked after children/young people may have needs which are more difficult to meet than others', outcome targets should not be set at a lower standard than those for their contemporaries

- Social Workers should act on behalf of the child/young person to organise resources

- LAC directs attention to everyday experiences and actions needed on behalf of children/young people to improve their prospects in adult life

- LAC must be perceived as a child-centred developmental way of working not an imposed bureaucratic system

- Assessment should take account of the perspectives of all those involved and pay particular attention to wishes/feelings of child/young person

- Positive action is required by staff and carers to improve children/young people's health and educational performance so as to enable each individual to develop her/his full potential

- Achievable objectives should be set for all dimensions of children/young people's development

- All plans should make clear who is responsible for what and by when

- Positive work is possible even in less than ideal circumstances.

Looking After Children: Good Parenting, Good Outcomes sets an agenda for good parental care by identifying the experiences, concerns and expectations of children and young people at different ages and stages.

The materials:

- Require those who are responsible for the care of children / young people to consider all aspects of their lives, not just those which have led to separation from home

- Require that plans for looked after children/young people are rigorously recorded and actioned

- Encourage partnerships between those responsible for the care of a child/young person eg. carers, social workers, families and relevant others

- Promote continuities in the lives of looked after children/young people and help to minimise the risks of disruption and multiple placements revealed by previous research

- Offer a comprehensive monitoring and review system for children/young people which meets the requirements of the Children Act 1989, and provide data which can be aggregated for management policy formulation, Quality Protects Management Action Plans and for statistical returns to the DH.

Benefits of LAC

For Social Workers and Carers

The system:

- Provides an agenda for work with children/young people
- Directs attention to the everyday goals of parenting
- Provides a means of assessing progress across a spectrum of developmental dimensions
- Ensures that all essential information is recorded in one accessible place and is regularly updated
- Strengthens partnerships between children/young people, parents, teachers and others
- Encourages reflection on the successes of children/young people not just their problems
- Raises sensitive issues
- Facilitates improvements in the quality of care which can be organised and provided for children/young people
- Rationalises documentation and creates consistency across agencies
- Provides a means of monitoring and evaluating practitioners' work which is likely to enhance levels of skill and facilitate career progression.

For Children / Young People

The system:

- Draws attention to their immediate and long term needs
- Provides a systematic approach to addressing their day to day concerns
- Makes it more likely that their views, wishes and feelings will be recognised, recorded and acted upon
- Provides a practical means of building a useful relationship with carers and social workers
- Creates a lasting life record which will offset some of the risks of multiple moves, support the development of a sense of identity and assist in the building of a sense of continuity

In essence, proper use of the LAC system greatly enhances the prospect of quality experiences throughout childhood (and beyond) for individuals.

Summary of Components of LAC System

Essential information Record (EIR)

An Essential Information Record(EIR) is designed to hold important personal information about a child/young person.

Part 1 provides information needed immediately by carers and should be completed before child/young person is placed.
Part 2 asks for more comprehensive information about background including legal and placement history.

Care Plan

A Care Plan ensures that all looked after children/young people have clearly stated objectives set out for their care and a strategy for achieving them.

Placement Plan

A Placement Plan is designed to outline the purpose of the placement in meeting the child/young person's identified needs.

Part 1: Placement Agreement includes the information and agreements which must be completed before a child/young person is placed.
Part 2: Day-to-Day Arrangements provides detailed information about a child/young person's everyday routines makes particular reference to health, education and identity needs and clarifies arrangements for contact.

Consultation Papers

There are three types of Consultation Papers:

- For parent/person with parental responsibility
- For foster carer/residential worker or independent visitor, and
- For child/young person

All are intended to provide the people above with an opportunity to have their views heard and recorded before a statutory review.

Review Form

A Review Form, following proper consultation and completion, informs the review process and ensures that:

- The overall Care Plan is still appropriate
- The placement and its agreed objectives continue to meet the child/young person's needs
- Work identified via the Assessment and Action records or otherwise to achieve agreed objectives is being undertaken

NB. In combination the above components meet statutory requirements for planning, placement and reviewing of children/young people looked after by local authorities.

They provide an integrated system in which, although there is some repetition of basic data, duplication is minimised.

Assessment and Action (A & A) Records

Six age-related Assessment and Action (A & A) Records promote good quality care by recording the development and progress of a child/young person across seven dimensions:

- Health

- Education

- Identity

- Family and social relationships

- Social presentation

- Emotional and behavioural development

- Self-care skills

NB. *No self-care skills are measured for those aged less than one year.*

9

Concepts & Definitions

Parenting

Parenting is an unconditional commitment and

- Carries responsibilities for the active promotion of a child/young persons welfare in the present and with a view to the long-term
- Continues in a modified form well into adulthood
- Involves mediating/advocating with respect to child/young person and the outside world
- Is affected by the characteristics/behaviour of child/young person
- Is not confined to adults who have a biological relationship with a child/young person
- Effective parenting (which research indicates leads to good outcomes for children/young people) requires:
- Management of conflict (even when parents are divorced/separated)
- Reliable provision of physical care and comfort
- Consistent demonstration of love and affection
- The ability of parents to see the child/young person's point of view
- The setting of clear limits, paying more attention to good behaviour than bad
- Spending time with children/young people and engaging in enjoyable activities.

Ineffective parenting (which in several research studies has been linked to unacceptable or anti-social behaviours) is characterised by:

- Lack of rules and clear boundaries
- Inconsistent discipline and empty threats
- Conveying dislike for the child/young person
- Ignoring good behaviour but punishing bad
- Lack of enjoyable shared experiences
- Harsh (especially physical) punishment leading to later aggressive conduct and low self-esteem.

Corporate Parenting

"The selfless character of parental love cannot be replaced or replicated" (Utting 1991).

"Corporate parenting" is a term which recognises public agencies' accountability for discharging parental responsibilities and that good results depend on children/young people receiving a range of inputs so as to help them fulfil their potential throughout life.

Whilst the high level of continuity of care experienced by most children/young people in the community may be difficult to match for those who are looked after, this is the goal for service providers as reflected in the objectives for Children's Social Services.

The term "Corporate Parenting" recognises that meeting the developmental needs of looked after children/young people requires co-operative working across agency boundaries.

The Looking After Children: Good Parenting, Good Outcomes
materials set out explicitly what reasonable parental care requires
in practice.

The Records focus the attention of staff and families on all
aspects of a child/young person's development including what
is going well for the child/young person and any difficulties
experienced.

NB.   *"The Government's Objectives for Children's Social
Services: Summary" and consequent expectations of
local authorities are summarised on page 16.*

Partnership

Partnership is built into *Looking After Children: Good
Parenting, Good Outcomes* at every point and many of the
questions contained on forms can only be answered by social
workers or carers working with birth parents or relatives or in
collaboration with other professionals.

Based on mutual respect, effective partnerships can be built
between people of unequal power providing the relationship
acknowledges and clarifies this inequality and seeks to
minimise it.

Partnership requires:

- Listening to users and carers
- Anti-discriminatory practice
- Agreements and recording of progress
- Providing sufficient information
- Honesty and openness
- Genuine participation

Outcomes

Outcomes (long-term consequences of interventions) may be
regarded as indicators of effectiveness.

With respect to childcare, at least five different kinds of
outcomes reflecting different perspectives can be identified:

- Child outcomes
- Family outcomes
- Professional outcomes
- Service outcomes and
- Public outcomes

"Child Outcomes" could include an evaluation of broad
measures such as the quality of an individual's functioning eg.
her/his relationships or acquisition of academic or practical skills
and/or of narrower more subjective ones such as how happy a
young person is with the results of her/his care experience.

"Family Outcomes" are more difficult to measure and
evaluate and need to recognise that there may be different and
sometimes conflicting interests within the family.

"Professional Outcomes" reflect the expectations the child
care staff have of their involvement. They should reflect the
objectives in planning for a specific child/young person and
may include not only eg. a changed living situation, but also
the processes and impact of achieving such a change.

Professional outcomes will tend to be seen as a reflection of
professional interventions whether successful or not.

Outcomes for all those involved may change over time.

"Service Outcomes" (or more accurately "outputs") will often be measured by means of statistics eg. numbers entering the care system or average time spent as a looked after child/young person. They need to be distinguished from outcomes for individuals.

"Public Outcomes" reflect the important, changeable and sometimes conflicting expectations of the public with respect to services for looked after children/young people.

Looked After

Children/young people who are looked after by a local authority may be "accommodated", "in care" or " remanded/detained".

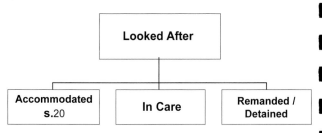

"s.20 accommodation" is a voluntary arrangement in which the local authority does not gain parental responsibility and no notice is required for removal of child/young person.

"In care" means that a court has made the child/young person the subject of a full or interim Care Order; this status provides the local authority with parental responsibility and (some) authority to limit the parents' exercise of their continuing parental responsibility.

The local authority has specific authority to detain those who fall into the third (non-voluntary) category who may do so as a result of:

- Remand by a court following criminal charges
- Detention following arrest by police
- An Emergency Protection or Child Assessment Order
- A "criminal" Supervision Order with a residence requirement.

Government's Objectives for Children's Social Services and Expectations of Local Authorities

The government has developed eleven main objectives which focus on better outcomes for children and clarify the role which social services should play in the achievement of these objectives.

A consolidated set of these objectives ("The Government's Objectives for Children's Social Services: Summary") was published in September 1999 and:

- Drew together material which had been previously circulated in separate documents, eg. National Priorities Guidance [LAC(98)22] and Quality Protects Framework for Action [LAC(98)28] and Performance Assessment Framework

- Introduced additional specific sub-objectives

- Enumerated fifteen Quality Protects performance indicators and nineteen Performance Assessment Framework performance indicators linked to the objectives

- Alerted local authorities to future "Best Value" indicators and a requirement for continuous improvement on the achievement of targets.

NB . *Amendments and addition s to current Quality Protects and Performance Assessment Framework performance indicators are planned.*

The government objectives are part of its wider social inclusion strategy which aims to tackle social exclusion and to provide better support to children and families through a wide range of initiatives.

Summary of Objective

Ensuring Stable, Secure, Safe and Effective Care For All Children

Objective 1. To ensure that children are securely attached to carers capable of providing safe and effective care for the duration of childhood by:

- Supporting families to help children in need be as successful as possible in their lives

- Ensuring more stability for children in the care of local councils

- Helping children who need them find secure homes with adoptive parents

- Making sure that, where adoption is the right thing, children in care are adopted as quickly as possible

- Make sure that, where long term fostering is the right thing, children in care are placed in long term foster care as quickly as possible

Protecting Children From Abuse and Neglect

Objective 2. To ensure that children are protected from emotional, physical and sexual abuse and neglect (significant harm) by:

- Bringing down the numbers of children who die as a result of abuse

- Stopping as much child abuse as possible

- Making sure that as few children as possible suffer from repeated abuse

Better Life Chances for Children in Need: good education, health car e and social care for all children

Objective 3. To ensure that children in need gain maximum life chance benefits from educational opportunities, health care and social care ("Children in need" means those children who need help from social services) by:

- Helping children in need to achieve more at school

- Helping children in need to grow up fit and healthy

- Helping children in need to keep out of trouble with the police

- Helping children whose parents are disabled or who have other health problems to enjoy a normal life

- Providing good quality care and treatment for children and young people with mental health problems

- Helping black and ethnic minority children in need to do as well as possible

Good Life Chances for Children in Care: good education, health care and social care

Objective 4. To ensure that children looked after gain maximum life chance benefits from educational opportunities, health care and social care by:

- Helping looked after children do as well at school as other children in the area

- Making sure that looked after children grow up fit and well

- Bringing down the numbers of looked after children who get in trouble with the police

- Making sure that black and ethnic minority looked after children are as successful as possible

Enabling Young People Leaving Care to Live Successful Adult Lives

Objective 5. To ensure that young people leaving the care system, as they enter adulthood, are not isolated and participate socially and economically as citizens by:

- Making sure that young people who were looked after when they were sixteen are studying, training or working when they are nineteen

- Making sure that SSDs are still in touch with young people who were in care aged sixteen, three years later when they are nineteen

- Making sure that young people leaving care are living in good accommodation at the age of nineteen

Meeting the Needs of Disabled Children and Their Families

Objective 6. To ensure that children with specific social needs arising out of disability or a health condition are living in families or other appropriate settings in the community where their assessed needs are adequately met and reviewed by:

- Making sure that local authorities and the health service have a complete picture of the numbers and circumstances of disabled children in their area

- Providing more and better family support to help disabled children and their families live ordinary lives

- Helping more disabled and non-disabled children use the same play and leisure services

- Giving children and parents information about the services which might help them

Better Assessment Leading to Better Services

Objective 7. To ensure that referral and assessment processes discriminate effectively between different types and levels of need and produce a timely service response by:

- Making sure that social services, health and education agree how they will assess what help children and families need and how they will respond

- Making sure that fewer families have to ask several times before their children get the help they need

- Completing the initial assessment within seven working days

- Completion the core assessment within thirty five working days of the initial assessment

- Providing services promptly in response to the assessment

Actively Involving Users and Carers

Objective 8. Actively involve users and carers in planning services and in tailoring individual packages of care; and to ensure effective mechanisms are in place to handle complaints by:

- Actively involving children and families in planning and reviewing the services they use, and in the decisions which affect them

- Ensuring that children in care have trusted people to whom they can speak and who will speak on their behalf to local authorities and to others

- Showing that children and families are becoming more satisfied with services

Using Regulation to Protect Children

Objective 9. Ensure through regulatory powers and duties that children in regulated services are protected from harm and poor care standards by:

- Making sure that all staff and workers stick to the rules which protect children and which set standards of care

Making Sure That Child Care Workers Are Fit For the Job

Objective 10. To ensure that social care workers are appropriately skilled, trained and qualified and to promote the uptake of training at all levels by:

- Making sure that all residential care workers are qualified to at least NVQ level 3 by March 2002

- Helping child care social workers achieve the new post-qualifying award in child care

Making Best Use of Resources: Choice, Effectiveness and value for money

Objective 11. To maximise the benefit to service users from the resources available, and to demonstrate the effectiveness and value for money of the care and support provided, and allow or choice and different responses for different needs and circumstances - by, for example:

- Making sure that every penny spent on children's services is used to maximum effect

- Meeting the needs of children and families from black and ethnic minority communities

Expectations of Local Authorities as Corporate Parent

In his letter dated 21/9/98 to elected Members, the then Secretary of State for Health and Social Services specified in Annex A that the government expects social services and education authorities to:

- Provide care, a home, and access to heath and education and other public services to which all children are entitled according to their needs

- Provide a mixture of care and firmness to support the child's development, and be the tolerant, dependable and available partner in the adult/child relationship even in the face of disagreements

- Protect and educate the child against the perils and risks of life by encouraging constructive and appropriate friendships, and discouraging destructive and harmful relationships

- Celebrate and share their children's achievements, supporting them when they are down

- Recognise and respect their growth to independence, being tolerant and supportive if they make mistakes

- Provide consistent support and be available to provide advice and practical help when needed

- Advocate their cause and trouble-shoot on their behalf when necessary

- Be ambitious for them and encourage and support their efforts to get on and reach their potential, whether through education, training or employment

- Provide occasional financial support, remember birthdays and Christmas or annual celebrations within the individual child's religion and culture
- Encourage and enable appropriate contact with family members – parents, grandparents, aunts, uncles and brothers and sisters
- Help them to feel part of the local community through contact with neighbours and local groups
- Be proactive, not passive, when there are known or suspected serious difficulties

PART 2 PRACTICE
Planning & Review Forms

Essential Information Record (EIR)

Purpose

The EIR form is designed to hold all important personal information about a child/young person.

A regularly updated EIR should ensure that care planning and reviewing processes are informed by accurate and relevant information and participation by key stakeholders.

Scope

Information is recorded under the following headings:

- Personal details
- Health
- Family details
- Education
- Legal status and child protection issues
- Placement history
- Professional contacts
- Administrative information

The EIR is in two parts which differ as described below.

EIR Part 1

Part 1 provides information needed immediately by carers looking after a child/young person and should be fully completed before s/he is placed

In an emergency, this form should be completed together with the Placement Plan, Part 1 [see page 32].

EIR Part 2

Part 2 asks for more comprehensive information regarding the child/young person's background including legal and protection issues and placement history

NB. *Certainty about the location of the birth certificate is vital since its absence may adversely impact on later plans/issues such as adoption, nationality, acquiring a passport or on fundamental issues such as identity if it transpires that key information, eg. date of birth, or details of paternity are different from those understood by the child/young person.*

Connections

A child/young person's EIR relates closely to the Care Plan and both parts should be updated before each review, on supplementary sheets if necessary.

Completion and Administration

EIR Part 1 is self duplicating so when it has been completed, before or at the time of placement, it can be left with the carer [see Common Queries appendix 2 for other possible recipients].

Wherever possible EIR Part 2 should be completed before the child/young person becomes looked after.

In the case of an emergency admission Part 2 should be completed as soon as possible thereafter.

Copies of a completed Part 2 should be sent to residential workers and carers with a further copy retained on child/young person's file.

Supervisors should help practitioners recognise and meet the challenge of updating the EIR having first discussed relevant issues with child/young person, parents, relatives and/or carers.

NB. *The "LAC Management and Implementation Guide" explains how responses to highlighted questions in Part 2 can be used to complete the SSDA 903 statistical return for the DH.*

Care Plan

Purpose

A Care Plan enables the identification of clear objectives for looked after children/young people and records the long term arrangements of achievement of those objectives.

A Care Plan is thus distinguishable from a Placement Plan, which details the arrangements for day to day care and assesses the role of the placement in meeting the objectives described in the Care Plan.

NB. *If a child/young person's placement is changed as part of an agreed plan or contingency arrangement it is usually necessary to amend only the Placement Plan.*

Scope

Background Information

In addition to recording standard personal information, eg. name, date of birth etc., the Care Plan form captures:

- History of contact/s with social services and support offered prior to this care episode
- Reason/s why child/young person needs to be looked after

NB. Reasons given here should correspond with those given on the EIR and guidance on the way reasons are commonly categorised is given in "Looking After Children: Good Parenting Good Outcomes Management and Implementation Guide"

- Alternatives to being looked after which were explored
- Details of the involvement of agencies and individuals in assessing the child/young person's needs.

The Plan

A number of questions within the sub-section referred to as The Plan address:

- The overall plan for the child/young person and reasons why this plan was chosen
- Identification and prioritisation of long term needs in a number of key areas in the life of the child/young person
- Type of placement being sought
- Length of time child/young person is likely to need to be looked after
- Agreements and arrangements in the event of disagreements
- Date of first review of this Plan

The importance of a contingency plan is also recognised so that if the preferred placement is not available or breaks down a crisis can be avoided.

NB. The development of a contingency plan may enhance understanding of placement support needs and reduce the probability of a disruption.

Connections

Where local authorities are seeking a public law application (usually a Care Order under s.31 Children Act 1989), the court will require a Care Plan in accordance with para.2.62 of Vol.3 of Children Act Guidance and Regulation Series and LAC(99)29.

Completion of certain questions on the Care Plan (together with others on the Placement Plan) provide the information required by the court.

NB. *The Guardian-ad-Litem appointed by the court for the child/young person will also wish to see the detailed plan prior to the hearing.*

The first review held is an opportunity to confirm or amend the initial Care Plan.

Completion and Administration

Wherever possible a Care Plan should be completed before a child/young person becomes looked after.

If this is not practicable it should be completed as soon as possible after a child/young person has been placed because it is important to be clear about the role which accommodation or care will play in meeting her/his over all needs.

A Care Plan can be changed **only** at a formal review which may therefore mean bringing forward its planned date.

NB. *Because the Care Plan links closely with the EIR it is important to keep the latter up to date.*

Copies of the completed Care Plan should be circulated to all those individuals identified within the Plan as having a significant interest.

Summaries of the Plan or notification of the arrangements made should also be sent to agencies consulted about those arrangements, and as applicable in accordance with the Arrangements for Placement of Children (General) Regulations 1991, or Placement of Children with Parents etc. Regulations 1991.

Placement Plan

Purpose

The Placement Plan is designed to determine how best a child/young person's day-to-day needs can be met during a placement.

It records arrangements for a child/young person's upbringing where responsibilities are divided between a number of people, eg. parents, social workers, foster carers, residential staff and young people themselves.

Scope

Placement Plan Part 1: Placement Agreement

This includes the information and agreements which must be completed before a child/young person is placed.

Part 1 incorporates the immediate agreements to accommodation and medical treatment and records essential names and addresses.

NB. *If placement agreements need to be changed this should be done on a new form.*

Placement Plan Part 2: Day-to-Day Arrangements

Part 2 provides detailed information about the child/young person's every day routines and clarifies contact arrangements

It should be completed jointly with parents and carers prior to placement.

NB. Any update of Day-to-Day Arrangements should be completed prior to each review.

Information in Part 2 : Day-to-Day Arrangements is recorded under the following headings:

- Routines
- Health
- Education
- Identity
- Contact
- Social and leisure activities

Connections

Where local authorities are seeking a public law application (usually a Care Order under s.31 Children Act 1989), the court will require a Care Plan in accordance with para.2.62 of Vol.3 of Children Act Guidance and Regulation Series and LAC(99)29.

Answers to relevant questions on the Care Plan (together with both parts of the Placement Plan) should provide the information required by the court.

Research has demonstrated that the health needs of children/young people who are looked after may be greater than comparable groups in the general population in both the short and long term. It is vital to take all practical proactive steps not only to protect but also to promote their health.

Arrangements to be noted here would include those for routine visits to a GP, statutory health examinations, continuing treatment for medical conditions, out-patient appointments with a specialist, future corrective surgery etc.

Research has demonstrated that the educational achievements of those who are looked after are worse both in the short and the long-term than those of children/young people in the general population. It is therefore vital to take all practical proactive steps not only to safeguard but also to promote the educational opportunities for these children/young people, eg. ensuring attendance by carers or social workers at parents' evenings.

Looked after children/young people often experience more changes of school than those who remain with parents or relatives so it is important to try to avoid any unjustified change of school.

Local authorities have a duty to try to encourage contact by children/young people with their families unless these have been restricted by a court order. 70% of looked after children return to their families within two years of placement and all but a few go back eventually. It is therefore important to promote links with families wherever possible, whilst understanding the need to provide support to all concerned in the process of contact.

NB. The table below demonstrates the scope and complexity of making contact arrangements

	Contact Where	How Often	At What Time	Supervised Yes/No	If Supervised By Whom	Face to Face	Other Means
Mother							
Father							
Brother							
Sister							
Others with Parental Responsibility							
Relative							
Previous Carer							
Independent Visitor							
Others Important to Child / Young Person							
Friends							

NB. Conscientious completion of LAC including Placement Plan Part 2 will facilitate the attainment of relevant Quality Protects objectives for individual children and young people.

Completion and Administration

In accordance with the Arrangements for Placements of Children (General) Regulations 1991, unless information is unavailable, all questions on Placement Plan Part 1 and Essential Information Record Part 1 **must** be answered and agreements signed by carers, social worker and, where appropriate child/young person and parent/s **before** any placement begins.

*NB. Part 1 may need to be filled in two stages, ie. the parental consent/agreement **before** a placement has been identified and the rest following its identification*

Wherever possible, all questions on Placement Plan Part 2 and Essential Information Record Part 2 should be answered **before** a child/young person is first looked after.

In the case of an emergency admission, they should be completed **as soon as possible** after a placement has been made and Part 2 of the Placement **must be completed within fourteen days.**

Day-to-Day Arrangements should be updated before every review and where they relate to a matter of some significance, be presented for discussion and agreement.

NB. *Arrangements will also need to be amended following decisions made at a review eg. contact arrangements.*

Consultation Papers

Purpose

Social Services can only fully evaluate the effectiveness of services if they ensure that there is a significant input from those who use them (children/young people), those who experience their effects (parents) and those who provide them (foster carers, residential and day care staff).

The Consultation Papers are designed to help children/young people, parents and carers to express their views, primarily for the purpose of statutory reviews.

NB. *Consultation Papers are just one method of trying to engage people more fully in the process of planning, decision making and monitoring the outcomes of interventions and must be seen as part of the wider picture of linking service provision to explicit professional responsibilities.*

Scope

Consultation Paper: Children/Young People

The Consultation Paper questions are central to all children/young people irrespective of age though the ability to think through and produce a written response to major life issues is age related. It would not be sufficient, for example, just to give a copy of the relevant Consultation Paper to a child/young person immediately prior to a review.

Feedback from children and young people has indicated that it is usually helpful if they are offered support and assistance in completing the Consultation Papers.

Children/young people should always be encouraged to attend their reviews, the most important function of which is to reach an understanding of their views, wishes and feelings and how they have developed since becoming looked after or since their last review.

NB. *Staff should think creatively about how the attendance of children/young people can be achieved either by communication via a third party, support for the child/young person within the review or via audio or video recording and chairpersons of reviews in particular must ensure that a child/young person does understand the format and processes involved. A National Children's Bureau publication "It's Your Meeting – A Guide to Help Young People Get the Most From Their Reviews" or "Children and Decision Making" by Nigel Thomas [details in bibliography] may be useful sources of ideas.*

Consultation Paper: Parent / Person with Parental Responsibility

Social Workers may not be directly involved in assisting parents to complete their Consultation Paper but should ensure that they have had enough time to consider their responses before filling out their papers.

NB. *The legal obligation to consult those with parental responsibility continues even where a Care Order exists. It is important for social workers to work with birth parents and help them to put forward their views or to ensure that someone else is available to do so.*

Consultation Paper: Foster Carer, Residential Worker or Independent Visitor

This explains that a review is a process in which carers or independent visitors, other people working with the child/young person being cared for, the individual her/himself and their family look at how things have been going over the last few months.

It indicates that important decisions may be made at a review meeting.

Foster carers, residential social workers or independent visitors should spend some time in advance of the meeting (using this form) thinking about and clarifying what to say and what changes they may wish to advocate to current arrangements or plans.

These individuals are encouraged to pass the completed form to the social worker **in advance** of the meeting.

The Consultation Paper advises that if the foster carer's, residential social worker's or independent visitor's attendance at the review is not possible, they should ensure that the social worker or someone else who will be there has a copy of the completed form or a tape-recording of their answers to all of the questions.

NB. *Foster placement link workers may be well positioned to assist foster carers complete this form.*

Connections

Chairpersons of review meetings should always ensure that children/young people are aware of the Assessment and Action Records and establish whether they have valued the process of completing them.

Completion and Administration

The Consultation Papers are designed to help children/young people, parents and carers to express their views, primarily for the purpose of statutory reviews.

The emphasis for work with younger children should be on addressing the questions and continually recording the responses in creative, age appropriate ways rather than expecting children to write them down.

NB. A social worker (or the young child) can use the spaces at the bottom of each page to add accompanying text and for very young children or those who have a profound disability using art as a support to expression can ensure that they are more than passive participants.

Older children/young people should be encouraged to regard the Consultation Papers as their chance to write down their views in an honest way and time must be given to discussing with them whether they need support and from whom.

Social Workers should encourage parents to return their papers **before** a review to allow time for professionals to consider their responses.

Review Form

Purpose

Reviews of looked after children/young people are a statutory requirement under s.26 Children Act 1989.

The **minimum** requirement is that a review be held within four weeks of an individual becoming looked after, within three months of that first review and subsequently at intervals not exceeding six months.

Only a statutory review can change a Care Plan. The first review is the opportunity to confirm/amend an initial Plan.

The purpose of the review is to ensure that the Day to Day Arrangements meet the child/young person's needs and that the overall Care Plan is still appropriate.

NB. *A review form contains confidential information which should not be shared without the agreement of the responsible authority and the persons concerned.*

Scope

Information and decisions are recorded under headings:

- Essential information
- Social worker's report
- Consultation and assessment
- Issues for discussion
- Record of discussion

- Review decisions
- Administration

Connections

The summary of work to be undertaken from the Assessment and Action Records is designed to be copied and attached to the Review Form.

The three Planning and Review Forms, ie. EIR Parts 1 & 2 and Placement Plan Part 2 should be updated before each review.

Care Plans and Placement Agreements should be completed on new forms if they need to be changed.

Completion and Administration

Consultation Papers for children/young people, parents and others with parental responsibility, carers and independent visitors should be sent out and completed (preferably before the review).

The Care Plan, Essential Information Record and Placement Agreement should be available at the review, together with a copy of the last review form.

The review form should be completed for each review, some parts before the meeting others at or immediately after it.

The Records

Assessment and Action Records (The Records)

Purpose

Assessment and Action Records are central to *Looking After Children: Good Parenting, Good Outcomes* as a system which monitors effectively children's progress and outcomes.

The overall aim of *Looking After Children: Good Parenting, Good Outcomes* is to improve the standard of care provided for looked after children/young people and to give them a better chance of achieving their potential and enjoying a satisfactory quality of adult life. This overall aim is reflected in objectives 1-6 of Quality Protects.

To achieve this aim, the progress of looked after children/young people is measured along seven developmental dimensions which are relevant to **all** children/young people. The tool used for this purpose is the Assessment and Action Record.

The Records are intended to help those professionally responsible for someone else's children/young people and have been designed to measure an individual's progress, assess standard of care and plan improvements.

Underpinning the developmental dimensions and use of the Assessment and Action Records described below, are concepts of parenting, corporate parenting, identity, partnership and outcomes which were explained in earlier sections.

44

The Records are based on two principles:

- That local authorities and other agencies caring for children separated from their families are accountable for the manner in which they discharge their parenting responsibilities

- Good results are dependent upon children/young people receiving a range of experiences that will enable them to fulfil their potential.

The questions in the Records are based on the best available research evidence and ask if things have been done which it has been found are likely to lead to good outcomes for children/young people.

Underpinning these questions is a belief that, given the significant numbers of people involved in parenting a looked after child/young person, there needs to be a formalised approach by relevant professionals so that the experience of the receipt of corporate parenting is brought closer to that of the child/young person living with their own (reasonable) parent/s in the community.

Six age-related Assessment and Action Records exist in order to:

- Promote quality of care
- Record quality of care received and progress across the seven dimensions of health, education, identity, family and social relationships, social presentation, emotional and behavioural development and self-care skills described earlier in this guide.

NB . *No self-care skills are measured for those aged less than one year.*

The following seven dimensions were initially chosen on the basis that "reasonable" parents would regard them as important (later confirmed in the research development phase) and the rationale for their relevance is summarised below.

Health Dimension

There is a growing recognition that good health can be achieved by the way individuals manage their environment, live and care for themselves though the way it is understood and undertaken may differ across social, cultural and national groups, caring for children's health is widely accepted as an essential parental task.

Working to improve children's health status is worthwhile not only in terms of its immediate benefit but also because evidence suggests that health gains in childhood last well into adulthood.

Health is inter-woven with and supports all other dimensions of a child/young person's upbringing and development eg. dental treatment can enhance appearance, self confidence, social relations and in consequence the achievements of the child/young person.

Most children/young people who become looked after come from disadvantaged sections of the population and are therefore at greater risk of poor health. Their level of vulnerability is further increased by high levels of trauma, stress, uncertainty and instability in their lives.

Although looked after children/young people experience more emotional and behavioural problems, research suggests they receive less professional psychotherapeutic help than their counterparts in the community.

Looked after children/young people from black and minority ethnic families may have specific health problems and those children/young people who have a disability or who have been abused often have additional health needs.

Looked after children/young people are a high risk group for many kinds of health threatening behaviours eg. smoking and drinking, sexually transmitted infections including HIV/AIDS and for girls pregnancy at an early age. A methodical approach by corporate parents to ensure the provision of health education, such as the LAC system provides, is critical.

NB. *The Department of Health are now monitoring and establishing targets with respect to children/young people looked after for more than twelve months, the percentage with up to date routine immunisations, percentage whose teeth have been examined by a dentist in the previous year; percentage who have had an annual health assessment in the previous year. There will be an expectation that all children entering public care have a health assessment, that the existing Personal Child Health Record is used (or a new one completed and kept with the individual) and that a personal health plan is developed to address both identified health needs and health promotion issues.*

Education Dimension

Given that educational attainments for a child/young person reduce the risk of unemployment as an adult, well informed parents award education a high priority.

Corporate parents should follow the example of a reasonable parent and recognise:

- The centrality of school to childhood in contemporary society,

- Its impact on quality of adult life, and

- The fact that its prime importance in care planning and work with children/young people has not, in the past, been sufficiently recognised.

The fundamental importance of literacy needs to be recognised since it becomes critical to the acquisition of other skills and knowledge and remains the first requirement of employers.

Looked after children/young people are at greater risk of not having favourable circumstances which would enable them to achieve sufficient literacy, ie. the close attention and support of an interested adult and access to books, computer and a quiet environment in which to use them.

Weaknesses in the essential liaison between education and social services and sometimes discrimination against looked after children/young people within schools can lead to unjustified exclusions with further consequences to learning, social relationships, risk of offending etc. These, in turn, may threaten a child/young person's placement.

The proportion of looked after young people who stay on in post-sixteen education is very low compared with the general population and unemployment levels relatively high.

In addition to educational qualifications and literacy which employers value, personal attributes such as punctuality, reliability, enthusiasm, initiative and a willingness to learn and get on with others, are also important and acquired through a combination of good parenting and a positive educational experience.

They are not easily acquired in disorganised families or in a series of care settings and concerted and consistent efforts need to be made by those fulfilling the corporate parent role to overcome such threats to the future employability of a child/young person.

NB. In order to bring the overall performance of those looked after for a year or more closer to local children, the Department of Health are now monitoring and establishing targets for the percentage of young people of sixteen or over with at least one GCSE grade A*-G or a GVNQ (and aim to achieve 50% by 2001 and 75% by 2003); the proportion of pupils who missed twenty five school days or more in the previous year; the relative performance at key stages; percentage achieving five or more passes at GCSE grades A-C as a ratio of local children's achievements and percentage of children/young people experiencing permanent exclusions.

Identity Dimension

Identity may be defined as "the individual's beliefs about who or what they are" (Tizard 1996) or "how someone thinks and feels about themselves especially in relation to other people" (Assessment and Action Records).

Aspects of identity include:

- Gender
- Ethnicity
- Religion
- Language
- Social class
- Age
- Sexual orientation
- Body image
- Relationship roles
- Personality
- Interests
- Occupation
- Personal history

Two central aspects of identity are **continuity** (feeling like the same person in spite of changes in appearance, aptitudes etc) and **uniqueness** (feeling distinct and different from other children/young people).

An individual has in fact many identities, some derived from group membership eg. gender, some from occupational and family roles eg. sister and some personal eg. individual values, attitudes and character traits.

Whether social or personal, all identities are mediated through social interaction.

Each component of a person's identity is evaluated by them and some or all may be held in high or low esteem.

Self efficacy (the sense one is competent and can solve problems) is related to self esteem and is also likely to be low in many looked after children/young people.

Major life changes can disrupt the ongoing constructive process of creating a "personal narrative" and threaten the sense of continuity.

Whilst acknowledging the multiple disruptions and loss of personal history and continuity often experienced by looked after children/young people, if these events can be given meaning the so called "personal narrative" can, informed by reliable information gradually be reconstructed in such a way that the threat to the sense of identity is minimised.

The Assessment and Action records thus represent a practical means of assisting even young children to understand their current situation and their history. They provide raw material which can help children/young people construct their identity.

Family and Social Relationships Dimension

Research in the 1970s raised questions about the State's ability to parent and highlighted drift and instability for children/young people away from home.

Given the significant risk within substitute care of placement change or disruption and the negative consequences which can last well into adulthood **all** sources of potential continuity - parents, relatives, schools and friends need wherever possible to be nurtured.

Research indicates that the need for continuity is most likely to be met by relatives such as siblings, grandparents, aunts and uncles or other significant people.

Evidence exists that children/young people who remained in contact with their parents tended to do better in the short and in the long term than those who had grown apart.

Recent research demonstrates that the great majority of children/young people eventually return home to live with parents or relatives.

Continuing contact with parents or the wider family is often a critical determinant of outcomes for children and young people.

Children/young people who find continuity of placement and attachments whilst looked after are more likely to achieve stability in adulthood and experience improved educational chances which in turn boost later employment prospects.

With a sound social network and a good family relationships the development of a secure identity is more likely with an associated reduction in health problems, ie. giving attention to family and social relationships within the Assessment and Action Records will help progress in the other six dimensions.

NB. *In pursuance of the objective to ensure that children/young people are securely attached to carers, capable of providing safe and effective care for the duration of childhood, the Department of Health is monitoring achievement of Quality Protects sub-objective 1.2 to reduce to no more that 16% by 2001 across all local authorities, the number of individuals who have had three or more placement s in one year. The percentage of looked after children adopted, the duration of time before adoption and the proportion of those placed for adoption but not becoming adopted in a given year is also being monitored.*

Social Presentation Dimension

Social presentation can be viewed as a combination of self presentation and social skills which are learned throughout childhood.

A reasonable individual or corporate parent will be as concerned about social presentation as about every other aspect of a child/young person's development.

Parenting styles in which social presentation is explained to children and young people and social processes and expectations are explained to them will support their achievement of developmental tasks.

Physical appearance affects how children/young people, especially adolescents, feel about themselves and they may be stigmatised because of an unattractive appearance, unlikeable personal habits or inappropriate social behaviours either by peers, teachers or by potential employers.

The Assessment and Action Records address the extent to which children/young people are helped by their carer/s and/or are learning to present themselves as:

- Well cared for
- Making appropriate choices about clothing and appearance
- Able to communicate effectively
- Able to behave appropriately in different contexts.

Emotional and Behavioural Development Dimension

The Assessment and Action Records:

- Provide the opportunity for carers and children/young people to record strengths and difficulties and therefore assess needs in this area
- Allow social workers and administrators to assess more easily the type and severity of difficulty experienced by the child/young person, to compare approaches to reducing the problem and thus to allocate resources efficiently
- Allow a systematic assessment of development over time and the outcomes for those children/young people who remain looked after for extended periods.

The main measures covered in this section of the Assessment and Action Records reflect the most common socio-emotional difficulties of childhood and adolescence which are:

- Feelings distressing to children/young people themselves (emotional problems including anxiety and depression)
- Behaviours unacceptable to others (oppositional, defiant and conduct)
- Overactivity and inattention
- Problems relating to adults (attachment and related problems)
- Quality of relationships with peers (pro-social behaviours)

NB. High scores on individual measures are only suggestive of the need for further action and do not provide a diagnosis.

As a group, looked after children/young people show increased levels of difficulty on all of the above measures, hence the importance of recognition and careful recording of relevant indicators.

Self Care Skills Dimension

Self care skills affect many aspects of a child/young person's life eg. her/his ability to cope outside the home, at play group or school etc and those who cannot adequately care for themselves may face ridicule from peers, have low self esteem and adapt less well to new situations.

While relevant skills will vary enormously according to age and ability, the issue of self care affects all children /young people.

For most children/young people the acquisition of life skills is a gradual process beginning in early childhood and progressing with age and development usually taking place in the supportive context of a stable family and other close relationships.

For the majority of children/young people, the process is also participatory, involving family discussions and negotiations, risk taking, making mistakes and trying again.

Looked after children/young people from disorganised families will often not have the benefit of making this kind of steady progress and gaps in their repertoire of skills may be further exacerbated by the movement and disruption of placements experienced by many.

For a young person, becoming adult can usefully be defined as a combination of a wide range of the following transitions:

- Leaving full time education and entering the labour market to achieve employment status
- Leaving family of origin to live with a partner or become a parent to achieve marital or parental status

- Ceasing economic dependence on family and becoming financially independent thus achieving consumer status
- Moving from dependency to an independent self identity
- Moving from family responsibilities for citizenship to political, civil and social independence thus achieving citizenship status.

The development of self care is essential to making the above transitions and achieving adult status.

In practical terms for older looked after adolescents the following skill areas are vital elements of overall self care ability:

- Budgeting skills, eg. shopping and managing finances
- Decision making and negotiating skills
- Practical skills such as cooking, cleaning and maintaining accommodation
- Diet and personal hygiene
- Managing relationships including sexual relationships

The relevant sections of the Assessment and Action Records provide the opportunity for systematising the processes and ensuring that children/young people are given sufficient support for them to develop the necessary self care skills.

NB. In pursuance of Quality Protects objective 5 of ensuring that care leavers as they enter adulthood are not isolated and participate socially and economically as citizens, the DH have developed and are monitoring achievement of a number of sub-objectives.

The sub-objective 5.1 includes maximising amongst those who left care at sixteen or over the number engaged in education, training or employment at nineteen and by 2002 to achieve a level of 60% of all young people of same age in a given area. The Department of Health are also monitoring the extent to which local authorities achieve sub-objective 5.2 - maximising the number of young people leaving care at sixteen or over who are still in touch with social services or a known and approved contact on their nineteenth birthday. The percentage of care leavers who, at nineteen, have "suitable accommodation" (sub-objective 5.3) is also being monitored.

Appearance

The Assessment and Actions Records are distinguished by age groups as follows:

Age Groups	Colour of Forms
Under One Year	Pink
One and Two Years	Violet
Three and Four Years	Yellow
Five to Nine Years	Green
Ten to Fourteen Years	Blue
Fifteen Years and Over	Aquamarine

Scope

On Records for younger children the questions are directed toward the carer. For ten to fourteen years olds and fifteen years and over, questions are directed to young people themselves.

Within each dimension the Assessment and Action Records include:

- A statement of aims
- Main and follow-up questions
- Plans for further action
- Responsibility for carrying them out
- An explanation for no action being taken
- Assessment of objectives
- A summary sheet which draws together actions to be undertaken with responsibilities and target dates.

NB. It is vital that this summary sheet should be taken to reviews.

Within each dimension a number of age-specific aims are identified which carers should encourage children and young people to meet.

A series of detailed questions establish whether children/young people are being offered the experiences which research suggests are necessary for their satisfactory progress.

Subsidiary questions ask respondents to note plans for further action where necessary and to decide who will be responsible for carrying them out.

The Assessment and Action Records can be used as:

- Discussion documents
- Planning tools
- Data gathering instruments
- Sources of outcome evidence with which to evaluate a service.

It remains the responsibility of the social worker / care manager to ensure that the Records are fully completed and that the appropriate people are consulted about the child/young person's development in each dimension.

The Records can be used as a tool to construct joint assessments to identify the extent to which objectives are being met in order to compare how a child/young person has changed between assessments. The Records can be linked to the Assessment Framework.

Social workers should use the information generated by the Assessment and Action Records to:

- Facilitate the development, maintenance and/or review of coherent, realistic current and future plans for a child/young person
- Inform discussions with their supervisor
- Demonstrate achievement of standards of practice
- Identify training needs.

Connections

The Assessment and Action Records are most valuable when completed as part of the planning and review system to provide a means for putting identified plans in to action and ensuring that identified needs are met.

The completed summary sheet should be brought to the review, the agenda for which then will be set partly by the issues raised during the completion of the Records. These identified issues may define who should be invited.

NB . *If issues of immediate significance become apparent during the completion of the Record, the review date should be brought forward.*

Completion and Administration

The Records will raise issues which may be very sensitive to many children/young people. It will often be more appropriate for the social worker to arrange for a foster carer or residential social worker who has a close or positive relationship to address relevant issues and complete the Record, along with relevant colleagues in health and education.

The summary sheet at the back of the Record clarifies what work needs to be done in each dimension, by whom and sets targets for its completion.

The need to maximise confidentiality of the information within the Assessment and Action Records, some of which may be very sensitive, should be recognised.

Whilst the summary sheets are required for use at reviews, the original version of the remaining contents should be kept securely on the file of the child/young person, with a copy made available to a residential unit/foster home if a carer is undertaking some direct work with the child/young person or given to the child/young person.

Frequency and Timing of Use of The Records

Although the planning and review forms enable local authorities to fulfil statutory responsibilities to all looked after children/young people including those in receipt of respite care, the Assessment and Action Records are primarily intended for use with children/young people for whom agencies have parenting responsibilities for a significant period of time.

Recommended timing is laid out in the diagram below.

At the four month review, arrangements should be made to complete the Assessment and Action Records for all children/young people unless a definite return date within the next two months has been agreed

Completing the first Record should begin immediately and the summary sheet checked at the ten month review.

The Assessment and Action Records should be used at the following frequency:

- **Children aged five and over - annually** plus additional check s on progress of work described on the summary sheets to be made at intervening reviews

- **Children aged under five** who are more vulnerable and experience more rapid developmental changes - **every sixmonths.**

NB. Good practice suggests the additional use of Assessment and Action Records at critical decision points eg. change of placement or after a disruption and especially before a final review in order to check that the best possible plans are being made in preparation for their leaving care/accommodation

When children/young people change placements within a local authority or move to new placements across boundaries, a copy of the most recent Record should follow them in order to preserve continuity of care.

Records should usually be completed within a six week period so that changes in the one area can be considered in the context of the changes in other dimensions.

It is important for the following timescales to be adhered to in order to maximise benefits from the system.

Frequency and Timing of Use of the A & A Records

For children under five

4 months after becoming looked after (second review)	Decide whether A & A Records will be needed
Between 4 and 10 months	Complete first Record
At 10 months (third review)	Present summary from first completed Record
Between 10 and 16 months	Complete second Record
At 16 months (fourth review)	Present summary from second completed Record
	Continue completing a new A & A Record every six months

For children aged five and over

4 months after becoming looked after (second review)	Decide whether A& A Records will be needed
Between 4 and 10 months	Compete the first Record
At 10 months (third review)	Present summary from first completed Record
At 16 months (fourth review)	Check progress on summary from first completed Record
Between 16 and 22 months	Complete the second Record
At 22 months (fifth review)	Present summary from the second completed Record
	Continue completing a new A & A Record every twelve months

Practitioners' Checklist

Do:

- Work **with** the child/young person to complete the Records and try to have a conversation about the topics raised, not a question and answer session
- Plan a number of sessions and involve the child/young person in deciding which section to do next
- Adopt the child/young person's perspective and talk with them in ways which they will understand and you will both find comfortable
- Use your own judgement, ruling out what is not appropriate and expanding on what is especially important to the particular child/young person
- Talk to significant others such as health visitors and teachers if appropriate
- Fill in the "Assessment of Objectives" at the end of each section; this is intended to provide a means of comparing how the child/young person has changed since the last assessment
- Aim to make sessions enjoyable for all concerned
- Use the Record to ensure high quality care.

Do not:

- Give it to the child/young person to complete alone
- Try to do it all in one session
- Do it all yourself
- Panic if there are gaps, but do plan how you will fill these in the future

- Justify the use of the system to a child/young person by saying that you have been told to do it
- Make promises you cannot keep
- Be boring !

PART 3 – MANAGEMENT

Benefits of LAC System For Managers and Supervisors

The system will:

- Provide an agenda for supervision and case planning
- Generate data for use by local managers in decision making and individual planning
- Allow tracking of care careers in a local authority
- Provide data that can be aggregated for service monitoring and planning and policy formulation
- Assist in the compilation of DH statistical returns, eg. SSDA 903, CLA 100 and Quality Protects Management Actions Plans.

Implications for Strategic Planning & Management

The most successful use of *Looking After Children: Good Parenting, Good Outcomes* appears to correlate with:

- The degree of commitment shown by elected Members, directors of social services and their senior managers, combined with
- A strategic approach which places the meeting of the developmental needs of children/young people at the core of all services provided to families.

The needs of children/young people within the looked after system are likely to be greater than those in the general population. A systematic approach to assessment, planning and review and the reduction of short-term responses can make a substantial contribution to the development of services and resources which are able to meet these needs and provide continuity of care.

Looking After Children: Good Parenting, Good Outcomes can be used to:

- Produce routine assessments of the developmental outcomes of looked after children/young people and
- Link such assessments to information about their needs and the services they receive
- Provide the means to plan more effectively for children/young people and improve their parenting experience
- Provide a framework for quality assurance, including compliance with current statutory obligations
- Underpin performance review processes
- Facilitate use of information to establish connections between need, activities, cost and outcome
- Contribute to children's services and strategic planning.

Responsibility for Sustaining The Benefits of LAC

Directors

Directors should ensure that:

- There is a consistent use of LAC documentation, especially the Assessment and Action Records

- The potential positive impact of LAC with respect to quality of recording and organisation of files is recognised and promoted

- Consistent day-to-day arrangements and long-term plans are being made for looked after children/young people and are regularly reviewed

- The LAC system is properly interfaced with other aspects of the child care system eg. child protection, disabilities and youth justice

- Mechanisms are in place for the engagement of health and education authorities in the use of the system

- The system is being used to improve consultation arrangements and to ensure that looked after children/young people and their representatives have an effective voice

- Links are developed with arrangements for performance review, local authority inspections of services and the children's services planning process

- Line managers use the materials and outcomes information generated to set supervision agendas

- Implications of LAC for human resource management or development are recognised

- Data gathered by staff is aggregated and used at a strategic level within the organisation
- Procedures exist to ensure accuracy and completeness of data and sufficient analysis and dissemination
- There is a local strategy for sustaining and developing the use of the system.

District Managers

District Managers should ensure that:

- The LAC system is being used consistently within their district
- Information from the LAC system is fed back to teams within the district
- Information generated by practitioners is being used by supervisors and team managers to inform their work
- Children/young people and their families are being involved in the using the system
- Opportunities for interfacing with other aspects of the child care system are developed
- New staff are given adequate opportunities to familiarise themselves with the system and its application within the district
- Training implications which emerge are recognised and addressed.

Team Managers

Team Managers should ensure that:

- Supervisors require their supervisees to evidence their work with looked after children/young people by reference to the LAC system
- The compliance level and quality of application of the system by team members is routinely monitored
- Decisions taken are dated and signed at appropriate places on case files.

Supervisors

Supervisors should ensure that the LAC system is used to:

- Provide the focus for supervisees to gather information and plan and review children's cases
- Develop coherent, realistic plans for children/young people's daily care and long-term future
- Identify training needs of field and residential social workers and of foster carers
- Provide objective information about the needs of looked after children/young people and how they are being met

NB. Supervisors may need to encourage staff to think beyond the mechanics of form-filling to the dynamic process it represents.

They may also need to remind them of the well established fact that when responsibilities for care are divided between a number of people, important parenting tasks can be overlooked unless they are written down and that this fact is the primary justification for the paperwork required.

71

Case Managers / Social Workers

Case Managers / Social Workers should ensure that the Records and Planning and Review forms are fully completed at relevant time intervals, that individuals have been consulted and involved and that the material generated is used to:

- Set an agenda for work with children/young people
- Strengthen partnerships between children/young people, parents, carers, social workers and others
- Direct carers' attention to the everyday goals of parenting
- Raise sensitive issues
- Identify where improvements can be made to the quality of care that children/young people receive.

Carers

Carers should:

- Encourage the child/young person to share in the completion of the Records and in contributing to the Planning and Review Forms
- If necessary, remind the social worker / case manager of the importance of use of the LAC system
- Ask for training and support to enable them to better understand and apply the system
- *NB. In practice, the most appropriate person to complete much of the Assessment and Action Record is likely to be the person/s who has/have day to day contact with the child/young person: i.e. the carer.*

Training Managers

Training Managers should:

- Ensure that **all** those who have a positive contribution to supporting *Looking After Children: Good Parenting, Good Outcomes* eg. fieldworkers, foster carers residential and administrative staff, managers and reviewing officers (and ideally service users) are provided with sufficient initial training to understand and support the system

- Establish a training strategy which will enable the identification of further training needs which may arise as the materials begin to be used eg. computer skills.

Connections with Wider Systems

Implications for Disability Services

The Children Act 1989 requires local authorities to provide services designed to minimise the effect on children/young people of their disabilities and to give them the opportunity to lead lives which are as normal as possible.

Work with children/young people who have a disability should be based on the principle that they are first and foremost children/young people.

The information generated by the Planning and Review Forms, and the Assessment and Action Records has the potential to provide powerful information to enable positive action to be taken to maximise opportunities for those children/young people who have a disability and avoid negative discrimination.

Short Breaks

For the many children/young people who receive short and occasional periods in care, the use of the Assessment and Action Records may not be appropriate. The Records can though provide a useful mechanism for synthesising the elements of what are sometimes complicated packages of care services from several agencies.

Use of the Assessment and Action Records is recommended by the DH in all cases where children/young people receive more than one hundred and twenty days of short breaks within a twelve month period (and will be of most value when completed as part of a planning and review system).

NB. See appendix 1 for flow chart of use of LAC with respect to short break.

The applications of the system as described below for emergency duty, youth justice, secure accommodation, pre-adoptive placement s and placement with parents etc extend beyond that set out in the DH Resources pack and reflects experience of best practice to date.

Emergency Duty

A significant proportion of placements are made outside office hours when the absence of many support services increases the risks associated with the looked after system.

Although admissions by emergency duty services sometimes have to be arranged with little notice and on the basis of incomplete knowledge of the individual's circumstances, the information and support requirements of carers are not significantly different from those in any other placement.

It follows therefore that even when a child/young person is accommodated out of office hours with no notice, EIR Part 1 and the Placement Plan Part 1 (the Placement Agreement) **must** be completed before a placement is made.

A Care Plan and EIR Part 2 **must** be completed as soon as possible and the Placement Plan Part 2 (Day-to-Day Arrangements) completed **within fourteen days**, with reviews being arranged if the placement appears likely to extend beyond twenty eight days.

Arrangements must be put in place to ensure that missing information is gathered and added to the forms as soon as possible.

NB. See appendix 1 for flow chart of use of LAC with respect to emergency duty services.

Youth Justice

Although remands to accommodation are often for a few weeks only, with many children/young people returning home following disposal of the court case, information and support requirements of carers are not significantly different to those in any other placement and some children/young people do in the event remain within the looked after system.

It follows therefore that even when a remand to accommodation is unexpected, EIR Part 1 and the Placement Plan Part 1 (the Placement Agreement) **must** be completed before a placement is made.

Though they may need to be modified to take account of the particular circumstances, a Care Plan and EIR Part 2 **must** be completed as soon as possible and the Placement Plan Part 2 (Day-to-Day Arrangements) completed **within fourteen days.**

Should it appear that the placement is going to extend beyond twenty eight days duration, arrangements **must** be made to convene a review.

NB. See appendix 1 for flow chart of use of LAC with respec t to remands.

Local authorities will need to determine and make explicit procedures about which of the tasks arising from these requirements are to be met by specialist youth justice workers and which by child care social workers.

Secure Accommodation

Local authorities have a duty to take reasonable steps to avoid the need for children/young people in their area to be placed in secure accommodation.

Because LAC highlights the developmental needs of an individual its use may facilitate these needs being identified and met before they become acute and less easy to manage.

The use of secure accommodation brings additional risks related to the close contact of very disturbed children/young people with one another, distance from home, reduced family contact, labelling etc.

Where a court has agreed that the use of secure accommodation is justified and made a secure accommodation order, LAC materials should be completed as for any other planned placement.

NB. See appendix 1 for flow chart of use of LAC with respect to planned accommodation. In what should be the very exceptional case of a child/young person being placed in secure accommodation directly by a local authority (seventy two hours maximum in a twenty eight day period) the placement should be regarded as comparable to one made by an emergency duty service and LAC materials completed accordingly.

Pre-Adoptive Placement

Because LAC facilitates the provision of high quality care and planning, it is also of value to those children/young people who are placed for adoption.

Although some modifications may have to be made, eg. with respect to contact and copying of reviews etc, completion of the relevant Assessment and Action Record will be a helpful guide for new parents as to key areas of a child/young person's development.

Placement with Parents Etc.

LAC is also of value to children/young people who are placed under the Placement with Parents Etc. Regulations and should be used.

During Care Proceedings where a child/young person may be placed at home subject of an interim Care Order, the EIR, Care Plan and Placement Plan Part 2 may offer clarification of important objectives.

NB. In Placement with Parents Etc. cases, completion of Assessment and Action records is more appropriately undertaken by the social worker in consultation with a parent rather than her/him alone. The information recorded may provide useful evidence of a child/young person's positive development or lack thereof.

Placement in Independent Sector

Local authorities will wish to include in their contracting with the independent sector standards which include the use of LAC material.

Many independent sector placements are some distance from a child/young person's home and the contribution of LAC in ensuring that the child's needs are addressed is considerable.

In addition, if a responsible authority needs to arrange for placement supervision to be undertaken by another agency, LAC will provide a high level of clarity as to the Care Plan and allocation of tasks to ensure its objectives are met.

Application to Children in Need & Child Protection

Many children/young people move in and out of care or accommodation and some will also be on the local child protection register.

In order to facilitate assessments, evaluate outcomes and analyse trends for such children/young people as well as those who may be in receipt of after care services, it is necessary to maintain comparable records for them all.

There is then considerable potential in local authorities developing a database for the wider group of "children in need" which is comparable to that provided by the manual LAC system or any of the computerised versions now available (see below).

The DH Framework for the Assessment of Children in Need and their Families includes references to the use of LAC.

Computer Applications

Software packages are currently available which will facilitate the local application of *Looking After Children: Good Parenting, Good Outcomes* and provide an efficient means of compiling statistical returns required by the Department of Health.

Further information on organisations which have developed packages is available from:

Copyright Advisor

The Copyright Unit (The Stationery Office)

St Clements House

2-6 Colegate

Norwich NR3 1PD

Statistical Returns

Looking After Children: Good Parenting, Good Outcomes generates a large amount of data about children/young people.

Aggregation of information about children/young people derived from the Planning and Review Forms and the Assessment and Action Records can not only inform a local authority about its own performance, but can also be used to compile the SSDA 903 and CLA 100 annual returns required by the Department of Health.

Information needed to complete the 903 return is entered in response to questions in EIR Part 2 indicated by the symbol 903

Word Processing Licence

Standard licences for producing templates for word processing the Essential Information Records, Care Plans, Placement Plans, Consultation Papers, Review Forms and the summary sheet at the back of the Assessment and Action Records are available.

These licences enable authorities to produce printed versions of the forms allowing multiple copies of the forms and thus:

- Enabling information about a child/young person to be updated more easily
- Overcoming difficulties of illegible handwriting
- Allowing flexible use of spacing and
- Enabling authorities to add logos or headings and questions that the forms do not currently contain.

Two licences have been proposed:

- A non-commercial licence for use by authorities wishing to develop templates of the forms for in-house use only, and
- A commercial licence for software houses or consultancies which are planning to develop templates on behalf of local authorities.

Further information may be obtained from the Copyright Advisor, details above.

Data Analysis Network

The purpose of the Data Analysis Network is to build on current research initiatives and to develop a service in partnership with local authorities and the DH, for the analysis and interpretation of data produced by the LAC system.

The Network is being planned as a number of regional centres each with an advisory group involving participating authorities and with an overall co-ordinating committee linking the centres.

Authorities which subscribe to the network will be offered both assistance with aggregating data for management purposes and an economic modelling methodology t hat will help them to link outcomes to the relative costs & services.

Further information about these proposals /costs to local authorities etc. may be obtained from Professor David Quinton, Centre for Family Policy and Child Welfare, School for Policy Studies, University of Bristol, 8 Woodland Road, Bristol, BS8 1TN, or Dr. Harriet Ward, School of Social Work, University of Leicester, 107 Princess Road East, Leicester, LE1 7LA.

Full time accommodation including remands, secure accommodation orders and short break care of 120 days or more

	BEFORE ADMISSION	AS SOON AS POSSIBLE	WITHIN 14 DAYS	WITHIN 28 DAYS	WITHIN 4 MONTHS	WITHIN 10 MONTHS
PLANNED PLACEMENT	Care Plan EIR Part 1&2 Placement Plan Part 1: (Placement Agreement) & Part 2: (Day-to-Day Arrangements)			Review Form	Review Form Commence A & A Record	Complete A & A Record Review Form
UNPLANNED PLACEMENT	EIR Part 1 Placement Plan Part 1	EIR Part 2 Care Plan	Placement Plan Part 2	Review Form	Review Form Commence A & A Record	Complete A & A Record Review Form

EDT placements and secure placements under 72 hour rule

BEFORE PLACEMENT	AT TIME OF PLACEMENT	AS SOON AS POSSIBLE	WITHIN 14 DAYS	WITHIN 28 DAYS	WITHIN 4 MONTHS	WITHIN 10 MONTHS
	EIR Part 1 and Placement Plan Part 1	EIR Part 2 and Care Plan	Placement Plan Part 2 (placement agreement)	Review Form	Review Form Commence A & A Record	Assessment and Action Record Review Form

Short break care for under 120 days

BEFORE ADMISSION	AT TIME OF ADMISSION	AS SOON AS POSSIBLE	WITHIN 14 DAYS	WITHIN 28 DAYS	WITHIN 3 MONTHS	WITHIN 10 MONTHS
EIR Part 1 and Placement Plan Part 1 and Care Plan					Review Form	Review Form

NB. *The tables in appendix 1 represent the minimum standard required and local authorities should attempt to achieve completion of relevant forms in all the circumstances described above.*

Appendix 2

Common Queries

Q. Are the *Looking After Children: Good Parenting, Good Outcomes* materials relevant to children with a disability, eg. in receipt of short breaks?

A. Yes, see page 74

Q. In emergencies, is it possible to reduce the paperwork required?

A. See page 75 for suggested modifications of the system in emergency situations

Q. Which forms need to be completed at a change of placement?

A. A new Placement Plan Part 1 & 2 will be required

A Care Plan **may** need to be amended if the case objectives have changed

EIR **will** need to be updated, ensuring that all recipients of earlier versions receive a copy. (One of the software applications of *Looking After Children: Good Parenting, Good Outcomes* can facilitate this process)

Q. Are local authorities allowed to photocopy the forms?

A. **Completed** forms may be copied. With respect to blank forms, see section on word processing licences

Q. Who should be given which sections of each form?

A. The allocation of the coloured sections of forms is for determination by individual local authorities and additional copies may be required

Forms	Copies to:
Essential Information Record, Part 1 & 2:	Carer; Foster Placement Link Worker (where relevant); Birth Parent; Young Person (in appropriate cases); Case file and Admin.
Placement Plan, Part 1 & 2:	Carer; Foster Placement Link Worker (where relevant); Birth Parent; Young Person (eg. 16+ year old); File and Admin.
Review Form (issues for discussion, record of discussion, review decision):	Child/Young Person; Mother; Father; Other Adult with Parental Responsibilities; Carer/s; Other Review Participants (if appropriate); Others Consulted before Review (if appropriate); Admin.

*NB. It may be appropriate to provide a copy of **all** of the review form to all the above individuals.*

Care Form	All those involved in drawing up the Plan and those with parental responsibility.

Appendix 3

Bibliography

- Looking After Children: Good Parenting, Good
  Outcomes Reader
  Editors Sonia Jackson and Sue Kilroe 1996 HMSO
  ISBN 0-11-321970-9

- Looking After Children: Good Parenting, Good
  Outcomes Management & Implementation Guide
  Editors Hilary Corrick, Debbie Jones and Harriet Ward
  1995 HMSO
  ISBN 0-11-321846-X

- Looking After Children: Good Parenting, Good
  Outcomes Training Guide
  Editors Sonia Jackson and Sue Kilroe 1995 HMSO
  ISBN 0-11-321884-2

- Looking After Children: Assessing Outcomes in Child
  Care
  Report of an Independent Working Party established by
  the Department of Health
  Edited by Roy Parker, Harriet Ward, Sonia Jackson, Jane
  Aldgate and Peter Wedge 1991 HMSO
  ISBN 0-11-321459-6

- It's Your Meeting - A guide to help young people to get the most from their reviews
  Ann Wheal and Ruth Sinclair 1995 NATIONAL CHILDREN'S BUREAU
  ISBN 1 874579 72 5

- Children and Decision Making – Nigel Thomas
  International Centre for Childhood Studies, Swansea

- Children Act Guidance and Regulations Volume 3 1991 HMSO
  ISBN 0-11-321375-1

Appendix 4

CAE Publications

- Personal Guides:
    - Children Act 1989 in the Context of the Human Rights Act 1998
    - Childminding and Day Care (England)
    - Child Protection
    - Residential Care of Children
    - Fostering
    - How Old Do I Have To Be…? (a simple guide to the rights and responsibilities of 0 - 21 year olds)
    - Domestic Violence (Part IV Family Law Act 1996 & Protection from Harassment Act 1997)
    - Looking After Children: Good Parenting, Good Outcomes (DH LAC System)
    - Crime and Disorder Act 1998 in the Context of The Powers of Criminal Courts (Sentencing) Act 2000
    - Sexual Offences Act 2003
    - Anti Social Behaviour

Available from: 103 Mayfield Road South Croydon Surrey CR2 0BH tel: 020 8651 0554   fax: 020 8405 8483 e-mail:

e-mail childact@dial.pipex.com

www.caeuk.org

Discounts for orders of 50 or more of any one title

Personal Notes